PEOPLE THROUGH HISTORY

PEOPLE ON THE MOVE

by Karen Bryant-Mole

WAYLAND

PEOPLE THROUGH HISTORY

People in the Country
People in the Town
People at Home
People at Work
People Having Fun
People On The Move

First published in 1996 by Wayland (Publishers) Ltd.,
61 Western Road, Hove BN3 1JD, England.

Edited by Deborah Elliott
Designed and Typeset by Chrissie Sloan
Cover designed by Liz Miller

British Library Cataloguing in Publication Data
Bryant-Mole, Karen
People On The Move- (People Through History Series)
1. Title II. Series
388. 0941
ISBN 0 7502 1661 1

Printed and bound in Italy by G. Canale & C.S.p.A

Contents

Cars	4
Bicycles	6
Fire engines	8
Motorbikes	10
Buses	12
Trams	14
Taxis	16
Ships	18
Planes	20
Trains	22
Coaches	24
Lorries	26
Ambulances	28
Glossary	30
Books to read	31
Index	32

Cars

A hundred years ago, there were very few cars on the road. For many years, only rich people could afford to buy a car. Today, roads are busy with lots of traffic. Most families now own a car.

1910s

Many rich people paid chauffeurs, like the man in the photograph, to drive their cars. Chauffeurs usually wore uniforms. They often had peaked hats.

1930s

Cars became cheaper to produce and more people could afford to buy them. The driving test was introduced in 1936. Before this, people could just buy a car and start driving.

Now

People use cars to take them where they want, when they want. Some families have more than one car. There are now so many cars that sometimes there are traffic jams.

Bicycles

Early bicycles were so uncomfortable that some were known as bone-shakers. Today's bikes are much more comfortable. Some bikes can be ridden over rough ground as well as on roads.

1880s

These bikes were called penny farthings. Riders had to balance very carefully. Special schools were set up so that people could learn how to ride them.

1930s

Cycling became a very popular sport. Lots of people belonged to cycling clubs. People also liked to ride their bikes out into the countryside.

Now

There are lots of different types of bike to choose from. Many bikes have gears which make riding easier. Most people wear cycle helmets to protect their heads.

Fire engines

Early fire engines were carts pulled by horses. People had to run or ride to the fire station to call the fire brigade. Modern fire engines race through the streets after receiving an emergency phone call.

1910s

These fire officers are wearing brass hats. They are carrying axes to help them break into rooms or buildings.

1940s

This fire engine could get to a fire more quickly than the horse-drawn cart. A bell on the top of the driver's cab was rung to warn people to get out of the way.

Now

Fire officers have to deal with all kinds of emergencies. These fire officers are clearing a flooded street.

Motorbikes

Today, motorbike riders have to wear crash helmets. In the past, a motorbike accident often killed the rider or left him or her with serious head injuries. Many motorbike riders now wear padded clothes, too.

1900s

This early motorbike looks very like a bicycle. It even has pedals and a chain. The rider has goggles to protect his eyes.

1920s

This motorbike has a side-car attached to it. The whole family could travel around together. A motorbike and side-car was much cheaper than a car.

1930s

Motorbikes were popular vehicles for women to ride. This rider is only wearing a beret on her head and ordinary summer clothes.

Now

Motorbikes are often used to deliver things quickly. A motorbike can be driven through town traffic jams much faster than a car.

Buses

Buses used to have conductors who collected the money for the tickets. Nowadays, passengers usually pay the driver as they get on the bus.

1900s

The first buses were pulled by horses. Most of the passengers sat inside this bus. Some sat outside, next to the driver.

1930s

All the passengers on these buses could travel under cover. Travelling by bus was a cheap and popular way to travel into and around the town.

Now

Today, lots of people make all their journeys by car. Fewer people travel by bus. Many bus companies now use small buses that are cheap to run.

Trams

Today's trams are powered by electricity. In the past they were pulled by horses. Trams run along rails. People use them in the same way that they use buses.

1890s

Trams were faster and cheaper than buses. They were faster because the wheels ran along smooth tracks and cheaper because they could carry more passengers.

1940s

If a tram broke down or had an accident, no other trams could get past. Passengers had to find other ways to finish their journeys. After a while, trams became less popular.

Now

Trams are appearing again in some cities. Many people are concerned about the pollution caused by buses and cars. Trams are quiet and do not pollute the air as they do not have petrol or diesel engines.

Taxis

Taxis used to be horse-drawn vehicles. Today, they are usually cars. Their name came from the taximeter which measured how far the vehicle travelled and how much tax, or fare, should be paid.

1900s

These taxis are waiting at a train station. They took passengers to work, to the shops and to their homes. Four-wheeled horse-drawn taxis were known as growlers.

1920s

This is a village taxi. Few villagers owned cars and there were not many bus services in the country. This taxi would have been faster than travelling in a horse-drawn vehicle.

Now

People often use taxis for getting around in busy towns and for going out in the evenings. People who travel by taxi don't have to worry about finding a parking place.

Ships

In the past, ships were the only way to make long journeys. Today, people can choose between ships and planes. Some people have special holidays, called cruises, on ships.

1910s

Lots of men worked on warships, like this one, during the First World War. It was the first time many of these men had been to sea.

1920s

After the war, some families decided to leave England. They hoped to start a new and better life in another country. This family is sailing to Canada.

Now

These passengers are on board a ferry. People use ferries to travel to the islands around Britain and to other countries in Europe.

Planes

Planes can travel long distances very quickly. Before planes, people usually travelled by ship. Journeys which used to take weeks by ship now take only hours by plane.

1910s

Most of the people looking at this plane would never have seen one before. Planes were an unusual sight.

1930s

Small passenger planes began making regular trips across to France. The air stewardess is pouring coffee from a silver coffee pot into china cups and saucers.

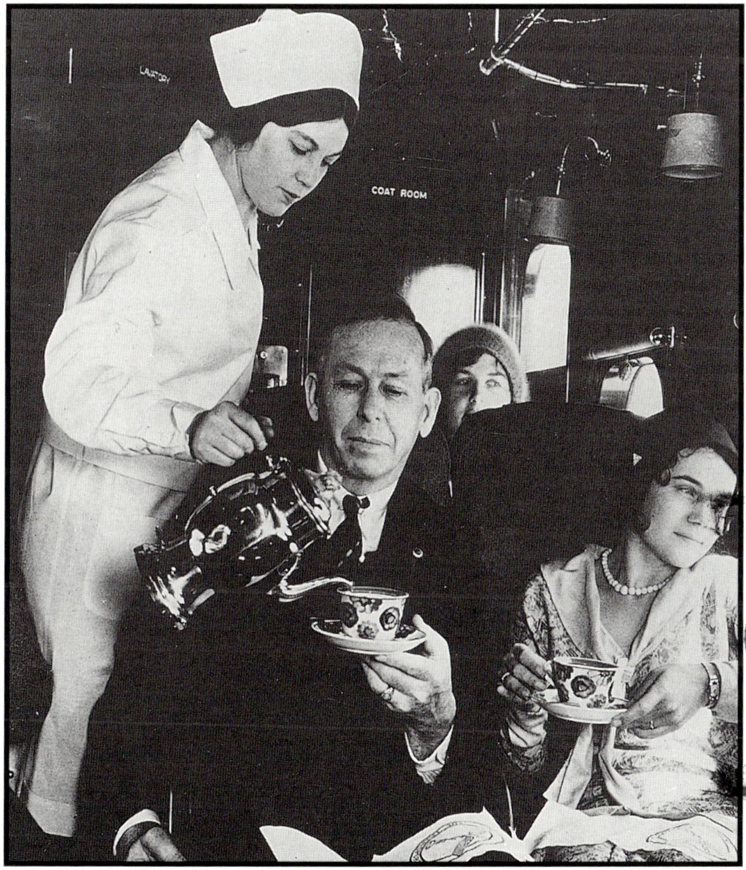

Now

Many people travel by plane on their way to holidays in Europe or the rest of the world.

Trains

Years ago, trains were powered by steam. Today's trains are powered by diesel or electricity. Steam trains still run on some private railways, as tourist attractions.

1910s

Working on a steam train was hard work. Coal had to be shovelled into a fire which heated up water to make steam. It was always very hot in the engine's cab.

1930s

These soldiers are on their way to a training camp. There were no motorways at this time, so it was quicker and easier to transport lots of people by train.

Now

Every morning and evening, the trains that travel in and out of towns are packed with people on their way to or from work. These people are known as commuters.

Coaches

Early motor coaches were called charabancs. The passengers usually travelled in the open air. Today's passengers sit in warm, dry coaches. Some coaches even have television screens.

1920s

These people are travelling into the countryside in a charabanc. Charabancs were often hired to take people on day trips. For many people, day trips were the only holidays they had.

1940s

These coaches took men to and from the shipyard where they worked. Factories often hired coaches for their workers, too. These coaches were sometimes known as works buses.

Now

This coach has an upstairs and a downstairs. It also has a toilet inside. Coaches are slower than trains or planes but they are one of the cheapest ways to travel.

Lorries

Today's huge lorries carry goods around the country and abroad. Years ago, lorries were pulled by horses. The driver's journey was slower and he travelled shorter distances.

1920s

Most goods were carried around the country by train. Horse-drawn carts, like these, were used to take the goods from the railway stations to the shops.

1950s

As vehicles and roads improved, more goods started to be carried by lorry. There were special cafés for lorry drivers which sold hot food and drinks. They were called transport cafés.

Now

Today's lorry drivers often travel long distances. Their journeys are recorded by a tachograph.

Ambulances

The first ambulances were simply used to carry sick people to hospital. Today's ambulances carry life-saving equipment.

1900s

Ambulances were often kept at Fire Stations. This horse-drawn ambulance has wooden wheels. They must have given the patient a very bumpy ride.

1930s

Many ambulances were manned by the St. John's Ambulance Brigade, who were people trained to do First Aid. They weren't paid, but gave up their free time to help.

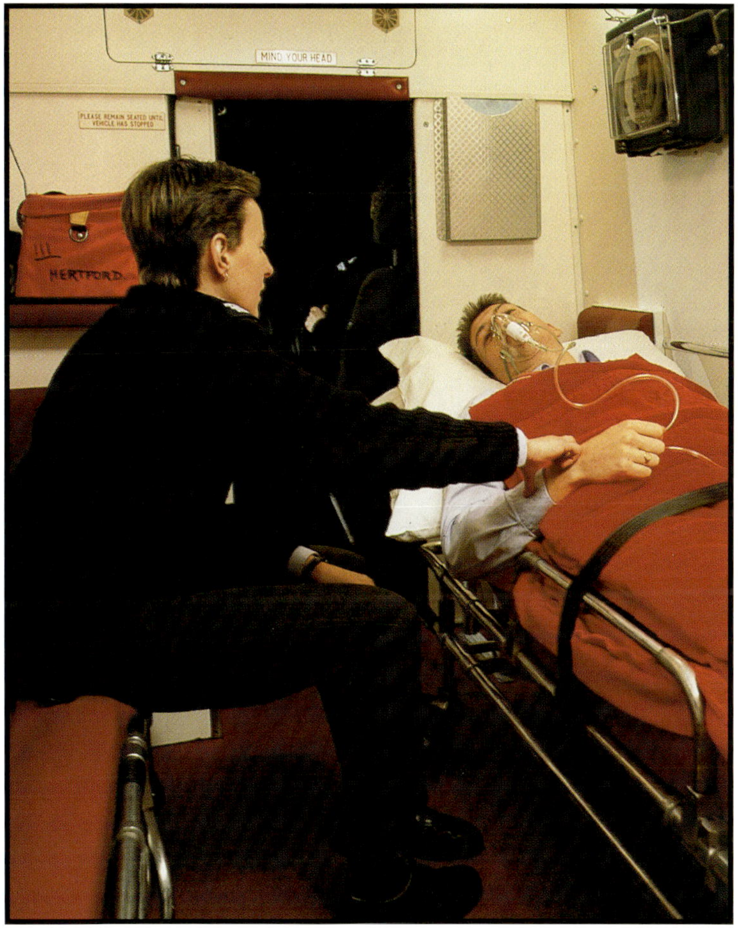

Now

Today's ambulance men and women are trained to deal with all sorts of emergencies. Their quick actions have saved many lives.

Glossary

beret	a soft, flat hat
cab	the front section of a vehicle, where the driver sits
conductor	the person on a vehicle who takes payment for tickets
driving test	the exam you take to get your driving licence
gears	a set of notched wheels that control how fast a bicycle's back wheel turns
goggles	strongly made glasses to protect the eyes
improved	got better
pollution	dirt in the air, water and ground caused by machines and industry
tachograph	a machine that records the speed and the travel-time of a lorry's journey
tourist attraction	an activity or place that people come to see

Books to read

History From Objects series by Karen Bryant-Mole (Wayland 1994)

History From Photographs series by Kath Cox and Pat Hughes (Wayland 1995-6)

How We Used to Live 1954-1970 by Freda Kelsall (A&C Black 1987)

Looking Back series (Wayland 1991)

Acknowledgements

The publishers would like to thank the following for allowing their pictures to be used in this book: Beamish, The North of England Open Air Museum 4, 5 (left), 6 (and cover), 7 (left), 8, 9 (left), 10 (both), 11 (left), 12, 13 (top), 14, 15 (left), 16, 17 (left), 18, 19 (left), 20, 22, 23 (left), 24 (and cover), 25 (left), 26, 28, 29 (left); Chapel Studios/Zul Mukhida, 5 (right), 11 (right), 13 (bottom), 25 (right), John Heinrich 17 (right); Eye Ubiquitous A.J.G. Bell 15 (right), David Bell 21 (right and cover); Hulton Deutsch 27 (left); Tony Stone 9 (right), 29 (right); Topham Picture Source 19 (right); United Air Lines News 21 (left); WPL (APM Studios) 7 (right); Zefa 23 (right), 27 (right).

Index

ambulances 28-29

bicycles 6-7, 10
buses 12-13, 14, 17

cars 4-5, 11
charabancs 24
chauffeurs 4
coaches 24-25
commuters 23
conductors 12
crash helmets 10
cruises 18

driving tests 5

electricity 14, 22
emergencies 8, 9, 29

ferries 19
fire engines 8-9
fire officers 8-9
First World War 18

growlers 16

holidays 21, 24
horses 8, 12, 14, 16, 26

lorries 26-27

motorbikes 10-11

passengers 12, 14, 15, 16, 24
penny farthings 6
planes 16, 20-21, 25
pollution 15

St John's Ambulance Brigade 29
ships 16-17, 20
side cars 10
sport 7
steam 22

tachographs 27
taxis 16-17
trains 22-23, 25, 26
trams 14-15
transport cafés 27